East Meets West

Cultures and Civilizations

Struan Reid

Thameside Press

US publication copyright © 2002 Thameside Press.
International copyright reserved in all countries.
No part of this book may be reproduced in any form
without written permission from the publisher.

Distributed in the United States by
Smart Apple Media
1980 Lookout Drive
North Mankato, MN 56003

ISBN 1-931983-34-8
Library of Congress Control Number 2002 141383

Printed in Singapore

Editor: Rachel Cooke
Designer: Simon Borrough
Series Consultant: Dr. André Singer
Specialist Consultants: Professor Denis Sinor and
Professor Thomas Höllmann
Maps by Swanston Graphics Ltd and Eugene Fleur

Contents

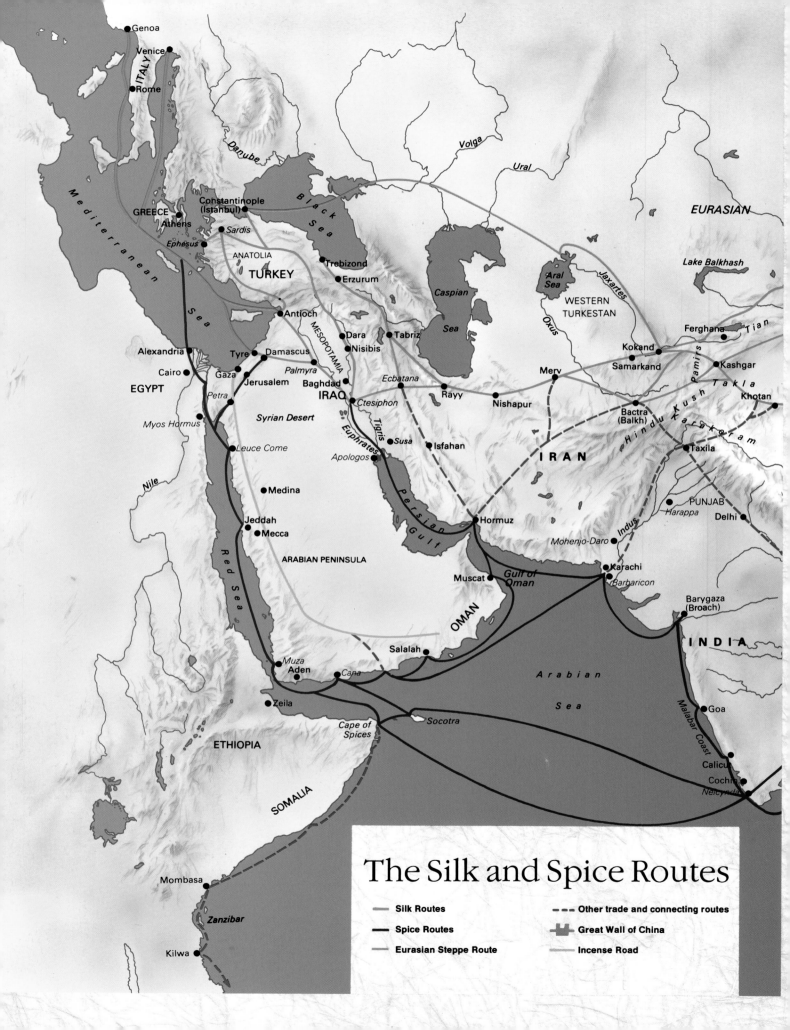

The Silk and Spice Routes

Genoa
Venice
ITALY
Rome
Mediterranean Sea
GREECE
Athens
Ephesus
Constantinople (Istanbul)
Sardis
ANATOLIA
TURKEY
Trebizond
Erzurum
Black Sea
Danube
Volga
Ural
EURASIAN
Lake Balkhash
Aral Sea
WESTERN TURKESTAN
Jaxartes
Caspian Sea
Antioch
MESOPOTAMIA
Dara
Nisibis
Tabriz
Ferghana
Tian
Kokand
Samarkand
Kashgar
Pamirs
Alexandria
Tyre
Damascus
Ecbatana
Merv
Takla
Cairo
Palmyra
Rayy
Nishapur
Khotan
Gaza
Jerusalem
Baghdad
Ctesiphon
Hindu Kush
Karakoram
EGYPT
Petra
IRAQ
Susa
Isfahan
IRAN
Bactra (Balkh)
Taxila
Myos Hormus
Syrian Desert
Euphrates
Tigris
Apologos
Nile
Leuce Come
Medina
PUNJAB
Harappa
Delhi
Jeddah
Mecca
ARABIAN PENINSULA
Persian Gulf
Hormuz
Mohenjo-Daro
Indus
Karachi
Barbaricon
Red Sea
Muscat
Gulf of Oman
Barygaza (Broach)
OMAN
Salalah
INDIA
Muza
Aden
Cana
Arabian Sea
Malabar Coast
Goa
Zeila
Socotra
Cape of Spices
Calicut
Cochin
Nelcynda
ETHIOPIA
SOMALIA
Mombasa
Zanzibar
Kilwa

Legend

—— Silk Routes
—— Spice Routes
—— Eurasian Steppe Route
- - - Other trade and connecting routes
▐▐▐ Great Wall of China
—— Incense Road

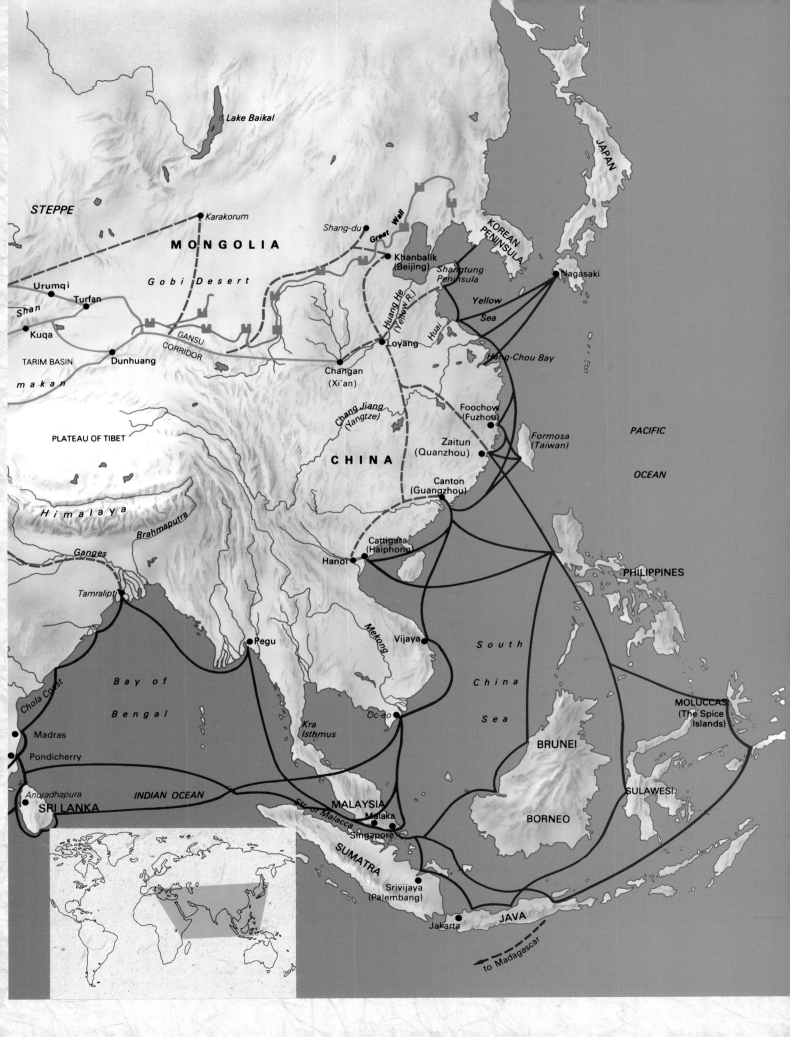

chapter one

Linking East with West

Trading Connections

▲ *A bronze incense burner of the third century B.C. from the south of the Arabian peninsula.*

▲ *The Great Goose Pagoda in Changan (modern Xi'an), China, built in A.D. 625, eastern starting point of the Silk Route.*

For thousands of years, the Silk and Spice Routes stretched across and round the vast continent of Asia. They linked its eastern lands with those of its west and Europe — the Silk Route by land and the Spice Routes by sea. They were trade routes. Along their many paths, caravans and ships carried precious goods. Spices and incense, silks and porcelain were some of the many luxuries of the East exchanged for Western commodities, such as silver, gold, woolen, and cotton cloth. There were huge profits to be made.

The Silk Route (or Road, as it is often called) refers, in fact, to several different land routes across Asia. The principal one originated in Changan (modern Xi'an), an ancient capital of China, and passed through the heart of central Asia to the eastern coast of the Mediterranean. Other routes joined it on the way: the Indian Grand Road, the Incense Road from southern Arabia and, in places, the Spice Routes. To the north, the Eurasian Steppe Route provided an alternative link across Asia, at times more popular than its southern counterparts. Although lesser land routes have existed before and since, the Silk Route operated as a major channel for international trade from about 100 B.C. to A.D. 1500.

It is harder to give the Spice Routes such an exact timespan. A network of sea routes from China to Indonesia, across the Indian Ocean and up the Persian Gulf and Red Sea has existed from as early as 2000 B.C. and ships still travel these sea lanes today. However, the routes that connected the Indian Ocean to the Mediterranean began to decline after the Europeans discovered the route east to India around Africa in 1498. It is no coincidence that this date is close to the time of the Silk Route's final decline. By sailing around Africa, Europeans could trade directly with India and the Far East, cutting out the middlemen of central and western Asia who for centuries had formed the backbone of the Silk and Spice Routes' trade. It is therefore the cultures and civilizations of the trade routes before A.D. 1500 that are the focus of this book, although the story continues right up to the present day.

For the Silk and Spice Routes were not just the means by which trade goods traveled between East and West, they were also channels for the migration of culture, while the wealth they generated encouraged the growth of civilizations. Along these routes, like links in a chain, a string of ports and cities grew up. In their market place, people of many different nationalities met to trade and exchange the ideas and beliefs that shaped their different cultures. These cultures might be expressed in the goods they had to sell — their designs, shapes, and color — or simply in their lifestyles — the clothes they wore, the food they ate, and the religions they practiced. Trading connections also encouraged people to employ skilled artisans from neighboring lands, which led to an exchange of technological skills as well as styles of art and architecture. By these means, the ways that the different societies along the Silk and Spice Routes lived and expressed themselves (their cultures) slowly changed, amalgamated, and developed.

▲ Resin from the myrrh tree is used to make incense. From ancient times, this was exported across Asia along the trade routes from Oman and Ethiopia, where myrrh still grows today.

▼ A Buddhist ceremony in Mongolia. Buddhism reached there by way of the Silk Route and has revived as the Mongols rediscover their old cultural heritage after 70 years of Communist rule, closely allied with the former Soviet Union.

Civilizations and Empires

▲ The empires of the Silk
Route around A.D. 100: the
Roman (red), the Parthian
(blue), the Kushan (orange),
and the Chinese under the
Han Dynasty (green). The
stability these empires
achieved enabled trade to
prosper and encouraged the
growth of civilization.

Civilization means literally "living in a city," although it has many other connotations. People first lived in cities partly for collective security, but partly because of the development of centers of trade. Large communities needed administration to regulate life, from water supplies to trading practices. These administrations financed themselves by taxes, which again depended on the city's success as a trading center. The growth of civilization is therefore inextricably linked with trade and with the Silk and Spice Routes.

▶ A party of Muslim pilgrims set out for the holy city of Mecca, the birthplace of Muhammad, founder of the religion of Islam. From the seventh century onwards, Islam has been a cultural focus for many of the peoples of western Asia.

But civilization also suggests cultural sophistication — a written language, advanced technology and science, magnificent buildings, and a flowering of the arts. These elements tend to be found during a period of peace and stability, a situation often brought about by a strong empire. In this sense, civilization is associated with the great empires of the past. The backdrop of expanding and declining empires against which the Silk and Spice Route trade took place contributed massively to the process of cultural exchange.

In the Far East, the Chinese civilization with its successive dynasties exercised the greatest influence on its neighbors. Despite many upheavals, this huge country was bound together by a shared language which resulted in the development of a remarkably unified culture. Two Chinese "golden ages" took place under the Han (202 B.C.– A.D. 220) and Tang (A.D. 618–907) dynasties — both notably associated with thriving international trade along the Silk and Spice Routes.

To the west of Asia, with Europe on its borders, there was a greater mix of cultures. From 500 to 330 B.C., the Achaemenid Empire of Persia (Iran) stretched from India to Egypt. It collapsed with the invasion from Greece of Alexander the Great, sending Greek culture deep into Asia. Later, power in Iran passed to the Parthians (170 B.C.–A.D. 224) and then the Sasanians (224–651), while the Romans superseded the Greeks as the dominant power around the Mediterranean. Frequent wars between the neighboring empires died not halt trade. Eastern goods were in huge demand in Rome and, later, Constantinople, which was the capital of the Roman Empire from 330 and also of the succeeding Byzantine Empire (610–1453).

The picture changed again with the sensational rise of the Arab Empire in the seventh and eighth centuries. Limiting Byzantine power in the Middle East, they drove right into central Asia. The Arabs brought with them a new religion, Islam, and this provided a focus of cultural development in the countries of west and central Asia for centuries to come.

In central Asia, home-grown empires, such as that of the Kushans (c. A.D. 70–224), had to contend with the expansion and decline of these successive empires. Despite this, the peoples of central Asia — the Kushans, Sodgdians, and the Turks, for example — devoted their own unique civilizations, greatly influenced by their central position on the Silk Route.

Throughout much of Asia, but particularly in the Steppe region to the north, there were many nomadic tribes. They were frequent traders and from time to time came together to form great military powers. One such power, the Mongols, succeeded in controlling almost the whole length of the Silk Route, a feat not equalled before or since. From 1260 to 1368, *Pax Mongolica* (Mongol Peace) saw a final flowering of overland trade between East and West. Ironically, a people that were not literally civilized contributed greatly to the civilizations to come — from China, to India, and Europe.

▲ *Roman aqueduct at Aspendos, western Turkey, part of the Roman and later Byzantine Empires. The aqueduct brought water from the surrounding mountains to the city on the hill. The Romans were skilled engineers and built on a monumental scale.*

▲ *A page from a Tang Chinese text of A.D. 777, when Chinese characters were often written in this elegant style. The Chinese had a written language from as early as 2000 B.C. and its use played a major role in the development of their remarkable culture.*

chapter two

The Culture of Trade

Traders by
Land

▲ *Tang Chinese pottery model, seventh to eighth century A.D., of a bullock and cart. One attendant is a foreign merchant, comically shown.*

▼ *Nomads gather in Afghanistan to buy and sell cloth. This kind of casual market has formed a focus for the nomadic communities of Asia for thousands of years.*

Empire building inevitably affected the trade along the Silk and Spice Routes. Political upheaval could make some of their paths unsafe but a way was usually found to continue the exchange of goods between East and West. A declining empire did not mean a decline in demand for exotic goods and the profits to be made were too huge for the merchants to be deterred from trading for any length of time.

Overland trade along the Silk Route was most liable to be interrupted by war and strife. Even during times of peace, it was not an easy highway to riches. Blazing heat, blinding sandstorms, and freezing cold were some of the hazards faced by the travelers and there was the constant threat of attack from bandits. Still many peoples' livelihood and culture evolved around the overland trade.

Goods were never transported by a single caravan or trader from one end of the Silk Route to the other. Different people conducted the trade along different sections of the route, and often particular racial groups became associated with its practice. The Chinese considered

trading a necessary but undignified pursuit and merchants had a low social status, so the eastern Silk Route trade was often handled by the empire's nomadic tribes. These tribesmen would then sell their goods on to the merchants of central Asia, for example the Sogdians from the area around the modern city of Samarkand.

The Sogdians played an important role on the Silk Route during the second to eighth centuries A.D. Although never empire builders themselves, they operated successfully under other powers, from the Kushans to the Turks, and the remains of their cities, houses, and art suggest that their merchants enjoyed a high social status, virtually equal to the landowners who ruled them. The Sogdian language, both spoken and written, was used in the conduct of trade eastward through to China and it was largely through this that new religions were introduced to China: Buddhism from India and Manichaeism from the Persian Gulf, for example. Religion played an important part in the traders' lives, whatever their nationality. Shrines were erected along the length of the Silk Route, where travelers could offer prayers for a successful journey and thanks upon a safe return.

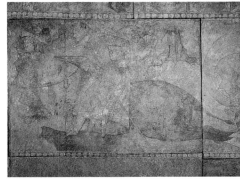

▲ *A charging horseman depicted in a fresco found in the Sogdian city of Penjikent.*

The merchants of central Asia would sell goods westward to Iranian traders or, at times, directly to Europeans via the Eurasian Steppe Route. The Iranians in turn dealt with the Syrians, Jews, and Greeks. Like the Sogdians, the Greeks were expert traders and had trading connections far beyond the area of their political influence. For many centuries, Greek and Farsi (Iranian) were the languages of trade on western paths of the Silk Route. Farsi is still very much in use today but the increasing influence of the Turkic peoples throughout northern Asia, culminating in the conquest of the Greek Byzantine Empire by the Ottoman Turks in the fifteenth century, led to Turkic languages replacing Greek and Sogdian as the Silk Route's common tongue. Today, it is quite possible for a Turkic Kazakh from China to communicate effectively in his own language in Turkey, thousands of miles away.

▼ *Panel from a portable Buddhist shrine of fifth to sixth centuries A.D. found on the Silk Route west of Turfan.*

Traders by Sea

As on the overland routes, the sea carriers of the trade goods changed at different stages along the way. The crews of the ships plying the Spice Routes were chosen because they were professional, skilled navigators who knew the routes and the dangers involved. The people of a particular journey were not always the carriers of that country's goods. For example, during the time of the Roman Empire, the Greeks traded on behalf of the Romans. Ships owned by Roman businessmen would be rented out to Greek merchants, often from Alexandria in Egypt, with knowledge of the Indian Ocean and the conditions of eastern trade. The crews would be composed of Greeks and any other seamen frequenting the Egyptian Red Sea ports. These ships could sail on the monsoon winds as far as the west coast of India. From the third century A.D., the Greeks' activities in the Red and Arabian seas were curtailed by the increasing power of the Ethiopian kingdom of Axum and Sasanian Iran.

Between the Persian Gulf and Oman and the ports of the west coast of India, Arabs (particularly Omanis) and Indians were the carriers, sailing in their own ships. The Arabs were to the Spice Routes what

▶ *A sixth century B.C. Greek vase with a sailor at its center and ships around its rim. The civilization of the ancient Greeks was partly built on their success as sea traders.*

the Sogdians were to the Silk Route — excellent long-distance traders who had the ability to adapt themselves to political change. They came into their own, however, with the establishment of an Arab empire and the rise of Islam. From the seventh to ninth Centuries, the Indian Ocean was a safe and rich ocean, crowded with ships of every nationality.

Ships that set sail from ports such as Hormuz and Aden could travel as far as China. They were manned mostly by Farsi-speaking crews, for the Sasanians had established Farsi as the commercial language of the western Spice Routes. The ships stopped at Muscat and other ports on the Omani coast, on their way out into the Indian Ocean. They traded their goods at ports of call all along the way, bartering with some people, using gold and silver coins with others. Slowly, they introduced their religion of Islam as well.

Until they had to compete with the Iranians and Arabs, Indians had acted as middlemen in the supply of western goods eastward to China. Through them, both the Hindu and Buddhist religions had passed to the peoples of Southeast Asia. Indian trading colonies were established in the rich port of Oc-eo and around the Malay Peninsula. In the China Seas, Korean sailors operated, often on behalf of the Chinese. During the Tang period, they formed a sizeable foreign group on Chinese soil, living separately in large sections of certain towns. At the same time, the port of Canton (Guangzhou) housed tens of thousands of foreigners, many of them Arab merchants and sailors from the Middle East. Zaitun (modern Quanzhou) was similarly populated in the thirteenth century, when Marco Polo and Ibn Battua, both famous travelers on the Silk and Spice Routes, visited it.

▲ An illustration from a 15th-century edition of Natural History by Pliny the Elder (A.D. 23–79). This work is an important source of information about the trade routes of this time (see page 36).

▼ View of the harbor at Muscat in Oman, one of the ports to grow up as a result of the sea trade. The fort above it was built in 1587 by the Portuguese who arrived relatively late on the Spice Routes.

▲ *The great khan of Qansuh-al-Ghuri in Cairo, built 1504–5. It is five stories high with the two lower floors used for storage of goods and the upper floors for apartments, rented by merchants and travelers.*

Cities of Commerce

Trade along the Silk and Spice Routes encouraged the growth of many cities, towns, and ports, for they were the centers where merchants met to buy and sell goods, or to replenish their supplies along the way. These cities would also be centers of commerce, providing bankers, credit and good supplies of money. If a local supply of metal was not available then it would need to be imported, encouraging further trade. During the Roman period, the Indian ports of Barygaza and Nelcynda imported copper, lead, and tin from the West to aid the local coinage.

A city that had a good position on the Silk or Spice Routes benefited in many ways. Taxes and duties raised on the goods that passed through its gates enriched its rulers and administrators. Many of its inhabitants relied on the trade for their income, some as merchants, others as organizers of finance or transportation. During the first few centuries A.D., the fortunes of the city of Palmyra in Syria were founded on its strategic position on the Silk Route between the Persian Gulf and the Mediterranean. It was known as a city of traders, its people operating many of the caravans that passed through the region. Pack-camels and ships can be seen carved on the façades of its splendid buildings, erected with the aid of trade-generated wealth.

The trade also provided a means of support for the producers of the goods to be sold: potters, weavers, dyers, glassmakers, and metalsmiths might all practice their craft within a Silk or Spice Route city's walls, safe in the knowledge that there was a marketplace for their wares. Cities would often become associated with a particular industry. For example, several of the cities on the eastern Mediterranean coast were famous for their dye works.

But at the heart of any Silk or Spice Route city was its marketplace. By the Islamic period, the bazaar of west and central Asia was like a miniature city. A network of covered streets (*suqs*) fanned out from a mosque at its center. Shops selling the same goods were always grouped together, so that there was a spice bazaar, a metalwork bazaar, a carpet bazaar, and so on. The most valuable goods were sold in a secure area called the *qaysariyya*. Beyond this lay the warehouses or *khans*, large square buildings with galleries and rooms for storing goods. Any Muslim settlement with a market also had at least one *hammam* or public bath, an institution inherited from the Greek and Roman worlds.

▼ *Sculpture of c. A.D.150 from Palmyra of the leader of a trading caravan. Behind him can be seen one of his camels. Many of the Palmyrenes were involved in trade.*

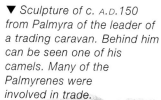

In the inhospitable countryside through which much of the Silk Route passed, travelers needed more frequent places of rest than the widely-spaced cities could provide. This led to the construction of caravanserais (palaces of the caravans), places where the travelers and their animals could be safe for the night and where they could be sure of food and water. Trading and changes of caravan teams could also take place there. Inevitably, some of these caravanserais developed into sizeable settlements in their own right.

▼ *Map of Constantinople (modern Istanbul) dated 1422 (before its capture by the Ottoman Turks in 1453). Situated at the mouth of the Black Sea, where Asia meets Europe, Constantinople was one of the major centers of commerce at the western end of the Silk Route.*

◄ *A 16th-century Persian manuscript illustration of a hammam or public bath, found in most Muslim towns and cities. Here, men could relax away from the noise and activity of the bazaars in which they worked.*

▲ *Panel from the Dome of the Rock, Jerusalem. Mosques are often decorated in this way. Geometrical designs were transformed into art by their Muslim creators.*

▼ *The mosque in Samarkand built by Tamerlane (c.1336–1405), who established a vast but short-lived empire. Samarkand was his capital and this building was a fine expression of its wealth and power. The huge arch, a feature of many mosques, was first used in Sasanian buildings.*

Building to Last

As trade encouraged the growth of cities and towns, their inhabitants sought ways to express their civic pride and sense of community. They also needed to show the status of their city, either as a power in its own right or as a part of a larger empire. Financed by the wealth the trade created, the citizens could best express these feelings through the construction of magnificent buildings.

Kings, princes, and governors built themselves palaces, as did the wealthier merchants. Streets were carefully planned and laid out, along with markets and bazaars. But the most important buildings for the whole community were their places of worship — the temples, mosques, or churches. These buildings displayed not only the strength of a community's beliefs, but also the success of its city. Their styles of architecture revealed a rich cultural heritage, incorporating local traditions with those brought by the religions they celebrated. The mosques found in so many of the cities of the Silk and Spice Routes are a good example of these various influences. They are often places of great beauty, celebrating the Muslims' love of God, and most lie at the heart of a city's bazaar (see page 14), indicating the central role that religion plays in everyday life. The basic layout of a mosque is much the same the world over. A covered area, often domed, is attached to a courtyard and most mosques also have at least one minaret, a tall tower from which the faithful are called to prayer. All have a niche (*mihrab*) in the wall of the covered area. This

indicates the direction of Mecca, the birth place of the Prophet Muhammad and Islam's most sacred city. All Muslims must pray five times a day, facing in the direction of Mecca.

However, as the religion of Islam spread along the Silk and Spice Routes, it was inevitable that the mosques should incorporate local traditions of architecture. The initial rise of Islam came with the expansion of Arab power in the seventh and eighth centuries. The first Islamic dynasty, the Umayyads (A.D. 661–750), built the mosque known as the Dome of the Rock in Jerusalem and another in Damascus. Both these cities had previously been held by the Christian Byzantine Empire and the two great mosques, built by local stonemasons and carpenters, have similarities with early Christian churches, particularly in their interior layouts.

◄ ▲ *Two interior views of religious buildings, but one is a church and the other a mosque. Left is the church of St. Apollinare in Classe, Ravenna, built in the sixth century. Above is the later Dome of the Rock mosque (A.D. 690–2) in Jerusalem, which followed the layout (but not the interior decorations) of the Byzantine churches typified by St. Apollinare.*

As the Arabs continued their conquest eastward into the old Sasanian Empire of Iran, the architecture of their mosques took on a more Eastern style. The great open arches that the Sasanians had built in their palaces were adopted into the surrounds of the mosque's courtyard, such as at the Great Mosque in Isfahan and Tamerlane's mosque in Samarkand. Sasanian design motifs, found on so many of the trade items of the Silk Route, were used in the intricate mosaics that decorated the mosques. Slowly, all these architectural influences evolved into the style that we have come to know as uniquely Islamic.

▼ *Stone statue of a bodhisattva (one who has achieved enlightenment) from Gandhara, which reflects the influence of Greek styles.*

Sculpting the Divine

The mosques of Islam may be beautifully decorated, but you will never find a person in their designs and no statues by the walls. Muslim law forbids the representation of the human figure in its art. This is in complete contrast to Buddhism, another religion to spread along the trade routes. Today its temples are full of statues and there is a rich tradition of Buddhist sculpture, with its remnants found throughout central, east, and Southeast Asia, even where the religion itself is no longer practiced.

Buddhism was founded in India during the sixth century B.C. by Siddhartha Gautama, the Buddha. Buddha means the Enlightened One and the religion demands the constant search for inner peace (enlightenment). This can be achieved partly through good deeds but also through prayer and meditation. Buddhist sculptures, which include images of the Buddha and scenes from his life, help the religion's followers in their search. The figures remind them of the Buddha's goodness and provide a focus for their prayers and meditation.

As Buddhism spread, different branches of the religion emerged with varying beliefs and practices, which in turn fed the development of particular styles of art. From the third century B.C., one style of Buddhist figurative sculpture emerged known as Gandhara, named after a region of what is now northern Pakistan. It was from this region that Buddhism spread into central Asia and eastwards along the Silk Route to China, so the style had a profound impact on the art that went with it.

The most distinctive feature of Gandhara statues is their combination of Indian and Greek influences. In 327 B.C., Alexander the Great had swept through this area, leaving in his wake many Western ideas. As a result, the Buddhist figures echo those statues of Ancient Greek philosophers and statesmen. The poses are formal, and the clothes are toga-like, draped, and pleated with high necklines.

The success of the Kushan Empire during the first century A.D. took Buddhism further into central Asia. Buddhist temples and stupas were built in many of the region's cities of this period, and the sculptural remains show the same Greek influences adapting to local styles. It

was a period of great trading activity along the Silk Route with China, so it is hardly surprising that Buddhism should begin to travel eastward as well. It is more remarkable that in the cave temples of the Tarim Basin, it is possible to find fourth-century Buddhist sculptures dressed in Greek fashion. These were carved by people who had probably never even heard of Greece.

As Buddhism reached China, its art encountered the strong artistic traditions of the Chinese. The rounded, fleshy forms (the Indian aspect of the Gandharan art) became flatter and more angular and, by the eighth century A.D., the clothes worn by the statues reflect the fashion of the Tang dynasty court rather than that of Ancient Greece. But the cultural links across central Asia to India that the shared religion gave are still clearly discernible in its art.

Above, the early Chinese figurine (A.D. 518) shows the change of style Buddhist sculpture underwent in China. The group below from the caves at Loyang is from the later Tang period.

The Sacred and the Secular

The process of evolution that can be seen in the sculpture and architecture of the trade routes is also found in their paintings and mosaics. The Buddhist cave temples of the Tarim Basin did not just contain carvings but brilliantly colored murals, showing Chinese, Greek, and Indian influences at work. Similarly, the influences behind the geometric designs and plant motifs of the mosques' mosaics could find their roots in Roman Byzantium and Sasanian Iran.

It was not purely in religious art that these influences could be seen, nor were the influences necessarily from a religious source. Secular art also flourished along the trade routes, particularly when successful trading links gave people money to finance its creation, and there was a constant cross-fertilization between art inspired by religion and that which adorned palaces and humbler city dwellings. The mosaics on the exterior of the Great Mosque at Damascus, which depict large scenes of architecture and trees, echo the style and images that can be found in some private villas in Pompeii, the Roman city buried by volcanic ash in A.D. 79. Conversely, the murals in the Sogdian city of Penjikent (near modern Samarkand) show hunting scenes and banquets in a way that is clearly influenced by the Buddhist traditions of wall painting.

▲ *Detail from one of the second century A.D. frescoes uncovered at Afrasiab (ancient Samarkand).*

▼ *Detail of the mosaic surrounding the courtyard of the Great Mosque at Damascus. The subject matter — trees, palaces, and pavilions — as well as style reflect those found in Roman and Byzantine art.*

▶ *Fresco from the Casa dei Vettii, Pompeii. Here is an earlier example of the same type of architectural façade, with trees seen on the Great Mosque.*

◄ *A painting of the Mughal Emperor Jahangir (1605–28) and his vizier. The flowers on the outer border reveal the influence of Chinese styles, while the inner borders are distinctly Islamic. Yet, as a whole, the picture is clearly in the Indian Mughal style.*

Although Muslim law forbade the depiction of the human figure in its religious art, there was no such constraint in other areas. The many Islamic manuscript illustrations in this book show the great popularity of this form of art. It was a tradition which founds its origins in Sasanian Iran — but the Mongol conquest gave it great impetus, introducing many Eastern influences. The Mongols established the Ilkhanid dynasty (1258–1336) in the territories of Iran and Iraq. They had close contacts with China, which was also under the Mongol rule of the Yuan dynasty (1264–1368). It seems likely that there were Chinese illustrators working in the Ilkhanid court. The influence of the more realistic and detailed style of Chinese artwork can be seen in the Persian manuscript illustrations from this period onward.

The increasing popularity of manuscript illustration in the Islamic kingdoms gave rise to another closely related art form, the miniature painting. These exquisitely detailed pictures were to become particularly popular in India, the idea carried there by the Mughals when they established an Islamic imperial dynasty in 1526. The Mughals were Muslims but claimed descent from the Mongol Khans and brought with them a mixture of eastern and western Asian traditions. Painting styles which originated in China 500 years earlier now surfaced in India to combine with those already present, and, most importantly, flavored with the strong Persian tradition.

chapter four

Precious Goods to Buy

Metal and Clay

▼ *Graeco-Bactrian silver coin of c. 220–190 B.C. It carries the portrait of King Euthymedes. The Greek influence can be seen in the lines of the hair and the facial features.*

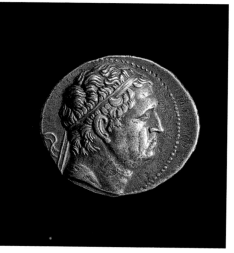

▶ *Small Chinese drinking cup made sometimes 730–35, during the Tang Dynasty. It is made in silver and gilt and the motifs it features, in particular the huntsman, show the influence of Sasanian metalwork.*

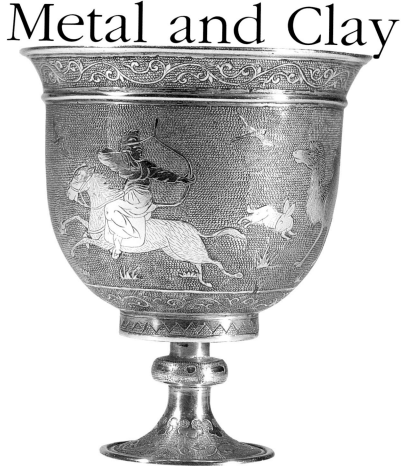

The expansion of great empires or religious conversion could bring about swift and often spectacular changes in a people's culture, which would be reflected in distinct developments in art styles. In large-scale art, trading connections alone were unlikely to cause such revolutions. However, the trade along the Silk and Spice Routes was responsible for a constant and very influential exchange of ideas, namely those expressed in the trade items themselves.

One small but vital item of trade that reflects these two processes is the coin. The Greek rulers that Alexander left behind in Bactria formed an independent kingdom from 250 to 139 B.C. They had a series of coins minted in the new Greek style, displaying exquisitely executed royal portraits on one side and Greek deities on the other. As these coins were distributed through central Asia, they inspired the minting of similarly-styled coins in neighboring kingdoms and those of later rulers. These were imbued with elements of their own culture:

local gods were substituted for Greek ones and the portrait style adjusted along the lines of their own traditions of figurative art.

The trade in precious metals did not just involve coins. The metalsmiths along the Silk and Spice Routes' paths produced dishes, bowls, and goblets to be sold in their markets. From the fourth to eighth centuries A.D., the metalwork of Sasanian Iran was particularly prized. The designs and motifs it featured were extensively copied by the metalsmiths of China's Tang Dynasty.

Under the Tang, China was wide open to new ideas and much of the craft work of this period reveals the impact of Sasanian exports. The Western habit of wine-drinking became popular and the shape of ceramic wine ewers and bottles reflected its foreign origins. However, the glazes and techniques of producing these vessels were uniquely Chinese and these, in turn, had a major impact on the West — for it was during the Tang period that Chinese ceramics began to reach western Asia in large quantities. Particularly admired was porcelain, hard but delicate and almost possible to see through. This fine "china" was so named in the West by its country of origin.

Porcelain was first produced in China in the eighth century A.D. but it was nearly nine hundred years before people in the West learned how to make it themselves. This did not stop them trying to imitate it, firstly in western Asia and later in Europe as well. The mimics used similar colored glazes over poorer quality clay and their products were extremely popular, although the much more expensive Chinese porcelain was still the ultimate in luxury. The blue-and-white glazes on porcelain, first used by the Mongol Yuan Dynasty, inspired many European adaptations, most notably the seventeenth century Delft ware from Holland. Even today, the famous blue-and-white willow pattern is still a popular design in Europe on cups, saucers, and plates.

▼ Nineteenth-century plate made at Worcester, England. The blue-and-white willow pattern is a direct descendant of earlier Chinese designs.

▼ This 15th-century Islamic scroll fragment is thought to show a Chinese trade or diplomatic mission to central Asia. Significantly, among the goods they carry is the highly-prized blue-and-white porcelain.

Weaving Cloth and Carpets

▲ *Fragment of Chinese silk from the Tang Dynasty period. The design of a deer in profile encircled by pearls copies that of earlier Sasanian silk designs.*

▶ *The Byzantine silk fragment found in the tomb of the Holy Roman Emperor Charlemagne. It was woven during the seventh century at the far western end of the Silk Route, at much the same time as the Chinese silk above. Although produced thousands of miles apart, both share the same design idea of an image encircled by a border that originated from Sasanian silk.*

The other greatly-prized Chinese product to be exported along the trade routes was, of course, silk. In the early centuries of the Silk and Spice Routes' history, China was simply known in the West as the land of "Seres," (silk) and the luxurious material became associated with the highest of fashions and the riches of courts. In China, too, the best quality silken cloth was reserved for the royal family and its weavers enjoyed a status as high as any painter or sculptor.

Production of both silk twine and cloth was at first exclusively in the hands of the Chinese, and even today the Far East is still the main producer of silk. However, around A.D. 300, silk twine produced in China was being woven into cloth across Asia, as far west as Roman Syria. The most influential silk-weaving industry was established by the Sasanian monarch Shapur II (310–379) in cities such as Susa, using the expertise of weavers seized during his invasion of Syria.

Sasanian silks were exported both east and west and their designs, themselves inspired by earlier Indian and Chinese work, incorporated into the patterns of the local textiles. Like the Tang metalsmiths, Chinese weavers borrowed Sasanian motifs, as did the Byzantine weavers of Constantinople and Antioch. There were two main types of pattern, one based on hunting or battle scenes and the other composed of circles each enclosing single birds or animals. The Byzantine silk fragment found in the tomb of the Holy Roman Emperor Charlemagne (742–814) combines both designs.

The Byzantine textile industry led to the spread of silk-weaving even further west. In the twelfth century, Roger II of Sicily brought silk-weavers from Constantinople to his capital at Palermo. This marks the birth of the Italian silk industry which still exists today. During the period of *Pax Mongolica*, when Chinese silks were widely available in Italy, the Italian designs were injected with more Eastern influences. The patterns became much more fluid, bigger, and bolder, with fewer heraldic animals in the Sasanian style. Scrolling leaf and flower forms were taken from the Chinese designs.

▲ *Iranian carpet, 17–18th centuries. It shows the layout of an Islamic garden design known as the chahar bagh. Trees surrounded by channels of running water provided coolness and shade from the blazing heat. Asian carpet weavers found inspiration for their designs from many different sources.*

◄ *A carpet salesman on a street corner in Abu Dhabi, capital of the United Arab Emirates.*

Silk was not the only textile industry to grow up along the trade routes. Carpet weaving was, and still is, of particular importance to many of the peoples of central and west Asia. Carpets rich in intricate detail adorn the floors of both the homes and mosques of these regions and a great mixture of influences can be seen at work. Islamic, Sasanian, Chinese, and Indian aspects may be detected, but in conjunction with strong local traditions. Each village and town developed designs that can be identified as uniquely their own. The earliest known carpet, discovered in the tomb of a Scythian nomad in the Altai region of Siberia, dates from about 500 B.C. It displays a mixture of Persian and Scythian influences, suggesting that the process of cultural exchange through trade was well established even then.

▲ Pushtooni tribesman dancing at a festival in Afghanistan. The belted caftan tunics worn with baggy trousers are characteristic of the region. Variations on this style of clothing can be found right across Asia.

▶ Sixth-century mosaic from the church of San Vitale, Ravenna, Italy. It shows the Empress Theodora (508–548) in a religious procession. The sumptuous clothes and jewelry of the Byzantine court can be seen clearly.

▼ The elaborate winter headdress worn by Kalash Kafir girls of the Birir Valley in northern Pakistan.

Shaping the Fashion

The silk and other fine fabrics, precious stones, and gold that became available as a result of trade along the Silk and Spice Routes had a tremendous impact on the clothes and jewelry people wore. The richness and variety of the materials and fashions worn are preserved in careful detail by artists who created the sculptures, mosaics, and paintings found in so many of the trading cities. The portraits carved during the second century A.D. at Palmyra show the elaborate hairstyles and jewelry a rich citizen would wear, as do the later fifth century murals found in the Sogdian cities of central Asia. Clothes and jewelry, like so many aspects of daily life, could express so much of a community's feelings about themselves — from pride in local traditions to a desire for the extravagant and the new.

However, for the vast majority of people, clothes were first and foremost practical, like the simple caftan. This long, straight tunic could be adapted to suit almost any lifestyle. Worn belted over pants, it was ideal for horseback-riding and was worn in this manner from the earliest times by the nomadic people of the Eurasian Steppe.

During the sixth century B.C., this style was adopted by the Chinese as they too began to ride horses, partly so that they could fight with the nomads on equal terms. The movement of the various nomadic tribes meant that, with modifications, the caftan developed as a useful article of clothing right across Asia, including India.

The loose-fitting draped Greek and Roman style of clothes also had its impact on trade-route fashions, as reflected in Buddhist art (see page 18). However, as the Roman Empire evolved into the Byzantine Empire, with its focus around the Balkans and the Middle East, so more Eastern fashions filtered through to Europe. Rich fabrics and jewels poured into the Byzantine capital of Constantinople and these were combined to form dazzling costumes that were copied far and wide. The Byzantine courtiers found the beautiful cloth, influenced by Sasanian designs, was better displayed by the straight line of the caftan rather than the folds of the toga. This style was also more dignified, which suited the image the courtiers wished to project, as did the increasingly lavish use of jewelry. In the eighth century, the power of the Byzantine Empire began to wane, but the costumes of its court became ever more extravagant, still proclaiming them as the great empire that in reality their armies could no longer sustain.

◀ *Sogdian mural from Penjikent, near Samarkand. The artist has given careful attention to the women's jewelry and hairstyles.*

▲ *Limestone bust of the second century A.D. from Palmyra. It shows a noble-woman heavily adorned with jewelry in a fashion that reflects the city's wealth as well as the mixture of Eastern and Roman influences it received.*

A Taste for the Exotic

▲ *An illustration from an Italian manuscript c.1385. It shows two women making pasta, the one on the right preparing the mixture while the other pulls it out into long threads. Italian pasta probably developed from the Chinese noodle.*

One of the most lasting effects of the trade between East and West is the evolution in peoples' diets, a process which continues today. The spices, which give the sea routes their name, added many new and different flavors to homegrown cuisines from China through to Europe. Black pepper, for example, came almost exclusively from southern India until the eighteenth century, yet it was used for flavoring along the length and breadth of the trade routes from before the birth of Christ. More staple components of people's diet evolved as a result of trade with rice and pasta both introduced to the Middle East and Europe in this way. Legend has it that pasta was brought back to Italy in 1295 by Marco Polo, but it was probably known long before this. Its origins may well stem from an even older Chinese noodle.

▶ *Two geisha women preparing the tea for a formal tea-drinking ceremony in Japan.*

▲ *Tang Chinese pottery wine ewer of the late seventh or early eighth century. It follows Western designs reflecting the origins of the grape wine which became a fashionable drink in Tang China.*

A taste for exotic foods was not always easy to fulfil as availability was limited and prices high. The diet of the nomadic peoples of the Silk Route was mainly a simple one, consisting mostly of meat from their animals. Even their alcohol was made from *kumis*, the fermented milk of their precious horses. Similarly, in China the Western taste for wine made from grapes became fashionable during the Tang period but it never began to replace the local rice and sorgum wines.

For many cultures, eating and drinking have ceremonial associations. A special occasion such as a religious festival is celebrated by a feast and the rules of hospitality mean that a visitor is greeted with the offer of drink and food. In Japan, a formal ceremony of greeting called *chanoyu* has evolved around drinking tea. Tea was introduced there in the eighth century A.D. by Buddhist monks and this religious aspect no doubt added to the significance of drinking it. Soon, it became popular in the Japanese court, where the qualities of different teas were discussed and poems even written on their virtues.

Tea drinking has produced many different customs in the countries that adopted it. Originally tea grew wild in northeast India but, at an early stage, it was introduced to other parts of east Asia. It was certainly being drunk and probably grown in China by the start of the Han Dynasty in 206 B.C. From China, tea was exported to Tibet. Here, it was drunk with salt and butter, and bricks of tea were even used as a form of currency. In the deserts of the Middle East, where tea was probably introduced by the Mongols, it was brewed with mint, making a refreshing drink in the scorching heat.

The expansion of Western European trade, particularly by the Dutch and English in the seventeenth century, helped promote tea drinking there as well. As an expensive foreign import, it was at first only fashionable with the very rich, and elaborate silver or porcelain tea caddies and teapots were made as a result. Today, in Britain and elsewhere, tea has become an essential part of everyday life!

chapter five

Words and Music

The Performing Arts

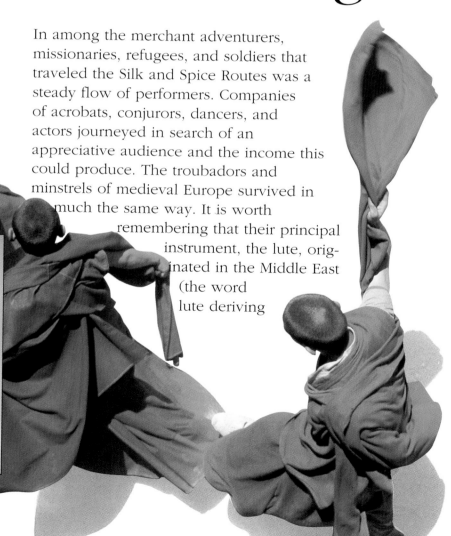

In among the merchant adventurers, missionaries, refugees, and soldiers that traveled the Silk and Spice Routes was a steady flow of performers. Companies of acrobats, conjurors, dancers, and actors journeyed in search of an appreciative audience and the income this could produce. The troubadors and minstrels of medieval Europe survived in much the same way. It is worth remembering that their principal instrument, the lute, originated in the Middle East (the word lute deriving

▲ *A Chinese pipa of the 17th century. The pipa was introduced to China from the West in the Tang period.*

from the Arabic *al ud*). This movement of people again resulted in the exchange and evolution of ideas and styles that shaped the performing arts of a particular culture, sometimes over great distances. The roots of *Commedia dell'arte*, the popular comedy and mime theater of sixteenth-century Italy, can be traced as far east as Korea and it, in turn, went on to influence many subsequent theatrical styles in Europe, including pantomime.

However, it was the Chinese that most welcomed the trading links as a source of entertainments and marvels. Performers were considered as much items of trade as any of the other goods arriving on the Silk and Spice Routes. The Chinese chronicles of the Han Dynasty reveal how the emperor took delight in acrobats and musicians from the West, and it is thought some performers may even have come from as far as Africa. This interest was revived during the Tang period, made stronger in the second half of the seventh century with the arrival of many Sasanian and Sogdian refugees fleeing the armies of Islam.

Whole orchestras, with singers and dancers, arrived from places such as Kashgar and Samarkand. They played flutes, harmonicas, gongs, drums, and various stringed instruments. The best known of these is called the pipa. It was introduced by the Sasanians and adopted by the Chinese, who in turn introduced it to Japan. Music from the Silk Route city of Kuqu appears to have been the most popular in China, particularly that played on a type of four-stringed lute. It was from this instrument that many Tang melodies developed. Musicians and dancers from central Asia were depicted on the Buddhist murals of the time, and the Chinese even buried small pottery figurines of them alongside their dead.

Indian music and theater reached China at this time via the Spice Routes and the Buddhist peoples of Southeast Asia. Orchestra and dancers from places such as Cambodia and Myanmar (Burma) performed musical pantomimes based on Buddhist stories like "The Peacock King." In the ninth century, some of these performers traveled on to Japan and versions of their plays are still performed by Japanese musicians and dancers today.

▲ A Mongol musician in traditional dress performs with one of the many stringed instruments used in Eastern music.

◄ Buddhist monks practice an exuberant religious dance.

Language and Literature

Alongside the music and dance, storytelling was another form of popular entertainment and a good story could find a place in the literature of many different peoples. A series of Indian stories called the *Panchatantra* has been found in sixth century Sogdian translations. The same stories were told throughout the Middle East and traces of them are found in popular literature of Medieval Europe, like tales by the fourteenth century Italian poet Boccaccio. Another example of this are the exploits of Alexander the Great, with tales of his adventures found in literature from Central Asia to Europe.

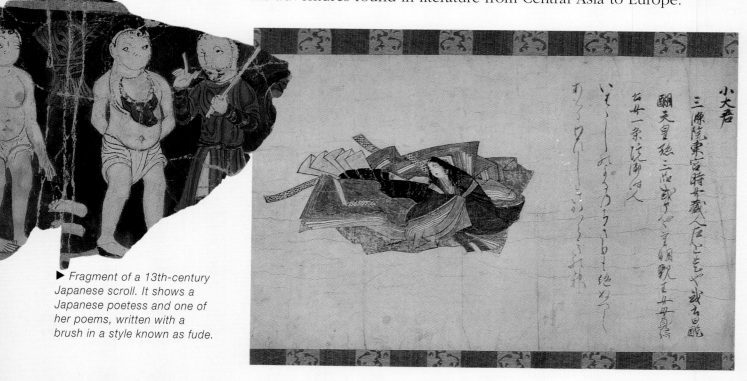

▶ *Fragment of a 13th-century Japanese scroll. It shows a Japanese poetess and one of her poems, written with a brush in a style known as fude.*

The same processes can be seen at work in much of early Japanese literature. The Heian period of Japanese history (794–1185) was a particularly rich period of creative writing. One eleventh century collection of stories, the *konjaku monogatari*, contains tales that originate from India and China, and the many short poems of the time, still considered some of the best in the Japanese language, reveal similar influences. This was perhaps not surprising in the light of the relatively recent arrival of Buddhism, with its Indian origins, to Japan by way of China.

An even greater reason for the Chinese influence on Japanese literature was that the Japanese script developed directly from the Chinese. At the beginning of the fifth century A.D., a Korean scribe called Wani sailed to Japan, bringing with him the art of writing. He wrote in Chinese and, at first, all records in Japan were kept in Chinese. For many centuries, it continued to be the language of officialdom and scholarship. The adoption of Chinese writing also introduced the art of calligraphy. Chinese phrases and Buddhist *sutras*, as well as Japanese poems, provided the material for this. Hanging pictures and scrolls were created with calligraphy — and the art of writing with a brush, *fude*, was developed by courtiers and scholars.

The way information is transferred through different languages, using translations and scripts, is an immensely complex one and results in some of the most interesting mixing and fusing of ideas and cultures. The sacred writings and scripts of the Manichean religion reveal this complexity. Founded in the third century A.D. by the prophet Mani from Ctesiphon, Manichaeism spread both east and west along the trade routes. During its progress eastward, the Manichean texts were translated many times from the original Aramaic or Middle Persian and versions have been found in Turkish, Pathian, and Sogdian. These translations include terms, phrases, and gods from the Iranian Zoroastrian religion as well as those from Buddhism. They reveal how the Manichean religion evolved, perhaps partly through the act of translation itself, adopting and adapting itself to beliefs already established in the lands it entered. One European sideline of this was a Manichean version of the *Life of Buddha,* which was translated into Georgian and then Greek as the saintly tale of *Barlaam and Josaphat.* In the fifteenth century, an English version of this tale was included in one of the first books to be produced by the printing press of William Caxton.

▲ *Illustrations from a copy of the 13th-century French poem* The Romance of the Rose. *An epic love story, it is full of images derived from the luxuries of Eastern trade, with noble lords and beautiful ladies adorned in exotic silks and jewels.*

◀ *Tomb figurine of the late Sui of early Tang Dynasty (sixth to seventh centuries) of a lady from central Asia reading a book with pages. This form of book was introduced to China during the Tang period but it only gradually replaced the scroll, the form taken by Chinese books until then.*

33

The Preservation of Ideas

The passage of ideas back and forth along the trade routes, whether concerned with religion, art, or more everyday pursuits, gave them immense dynamism and vitality. As we have seen throughout this book, ideas were constantly developing, adding to, or taking on aspects of the local traditions they encountered. Besides this, there was a large element of preservation of beliefs and ideas that might otherwise have been lost. For example, by the fifth century A.D., Buddhism had virtually died out in northern India where it originated but its expansion to other areas, such as China and Southeast Asia, guaranteed its survival right up to the present day.

These two processes are also seen at work in the history of philosophy — the study of all these ideas and how we arrive at them. The term philosophy comes from a Greek word meaning "love of wisdom" and it is to Ancient Greece that the roots of Western philosophy are traced. Here, scholars, or rather philosophers, studied many subjects, among them science and mathematics, but they also asked questions about the nature of human existence and

▼ *Marble head of the Greek philosopher Aristotle, at one stage tutor to Alexander the Great. Aristotle's philosophy, which stressed the importance of reason and moderation, became the foundation of Islamic philosophy.*

▶ *Florence, Italy, once center of the European Renaissance. During this period, the learning of ancient Greece and Rome was rediscovered, partly through increased trading contacts with the Arab world.*

the universe as a whole. The answers provided by the great philosophers — Socrates (469–399 B.C.), Plato (429–347 B.C.), and Aristotle (384–322 B.C.) — helped shape many systems of thought in the West, from politics to Christian doctrine. The methods of asking the right questions, of debate and argument, that they established are still studied as part of philosophy today.

However, this important legacy was not simply passed down by Europeans over the centuries. Much of it would have been lost but for the work of Islamic scholars. From the seventh century A.D., the expanding Arab Empire absorbed many of the scientific and philosophical ideas from its new territories, especially those of the Byzantine Greeks (inheritors of Greek and Roman learning). Intellectual activity flourished in this new empire. Some of the Greek methods of teaching and debate were adopted and translations of important books undertaken. During the reign of Caliph al-Ma'mun (813–33), a special school was founded purely for the purpose of translation. It was called the *Bayt al-hikma* (The House of Wisdom).

The translations of the Greek philosophers were read and taught in Islamic schools, but Islam also produced its own philosophers. Two of the greatest were al-Farabi (died 950) and Ibn-Sina (980–1037), known in the West as Avicenna. The work of these men and others did not simply transmit the Greek ideas but greatly extended their range. As European scholars began to discover their Classical past in the Medieval and Renaissance periods, partly through the Arabic translations, they also took on the developments made by these Islamic philosophers.

▲ Stone bust of the Greek philosopher Plato, pupil of Socrates and tutor to Aristotle. His works, which had a profound influence on Christianity and European culture, were partly preserved through Arabic translations.

◀ An illustration of an Islamic public library. These were centers of study where local and visiting scholars could gather to exchange views. Discussions of philosophy, both ancient and new, would have formed much of their debate.

chapter six

European Images of the East

Travelers' Tales

▼ *Engraving from a book entitled China published in 1667. It shows a Chinaman about to kill two giant serpents. The whole illustration projects the European idea of China as a strange landscape populated by fantastic plants and animals.*

From the earliest times, Europe had direct contact with the neighboring peoples of Western Asia. At various stages, too, European empires held substantial territories in Asia — firstly from the staggering conquests of Alexander the Great to the later holdings of Rome and Byzantium. However, further east, European knowledge of Asia became increasingly limited. Few had traveled very far eastward and even fewer left any record of their journey. As a result, the Western image of the Orient was based partly on fact but largely on fiction, probably fed on the tales of western Asians. They were keen to protect their lucrative role as the middlemen of the trade routes and to endow their goods with an element of mystery and marvel.

One of the first European accounts of the lands in the East was written by Megasthenes, a Greek ambassador sent to the Maurya kingdom of northern Indian in 303 B.C. His book, entitled *Indica*, contained information about the people, customs, and natural history of the area. But he also included a number of fables, such as a description of the "umbrella-foots," one-legged people whose single foot was so large they could use it as a sunshade. This description and others were later borrowed by the Roman scholar Pliny the Elder (A.D. 23–79) when he compiled his monumental *Natural History*.

Pliny's work also included some description of the people of Seres (the Chinese), as did *The Periplus of the Erythraeum Sea,* a document on the Spice Route trade. It was written around A.D. 80, probably by a Greek sea captain. Both books idealized the Chinese, seeing them as peace-loving and taciturn. An image also emerged at this time of the ruler of China being strict but absolutely fair, a myth that continued to be widely believed for many centuries. Boccaccio made use of it and, even later, the French philosopher, Voltaire (1694–1778).

From the seventh century, the strength of the Islamic empires created an effective barrier between Europe and the East. However, the rise of Mongol power in the thirteenth century enabled Europeans to travel to China for the first time. Most famously, Marco Polo traveled east to trade and his account of his journey from 1271–95 is now regarded as one of the most important, and accurate, sources of information on the East of this time.

▲ *Map of Asia, engraved in 1562 by Jenkinson. It was based on Marco Polo's account of his travels, which were by then over 250 years old.*

◄ *Illustration from the* Livre des Merveilles, *a 15th-century French version of Marco Polo's travels. It incorporated the extraordinary beings and marvels of other accounts that appealed to the popular imagination.*

His book was extremely popular in Medieval and Renaissance Europe, but it was its more bizarre elements that inspired people's imaginations. Equally popular were such fantastic accounts epitomized by *The Travels of Sir John Mandeville.* It was 500 years before it was discovered that Sir John had never traveled and his "personal experiences" were pure invention — but this book supplied the stories people wanted to hear. Borrowing ideas from Pliny and Megasthenes, the author described an Orient filled with strange monster-people, some with eyes in their foreheads and others without heads at all. It was no wonder that Europeans regarded the East through a veil of fantasy, seeing a place filled with exotic people and strange customs.

Styles of the Orient

▲ *English mahogany bed designed by Thomas Chippendale (c.1718–79). His design clearly shows the European "chinoiserie" style, with its dragons, upswept lines, and "bamboo" effect.*

▼ *Engraving by M. Aubert from a painting by Jean Watteau. Watteau painted many fanciful scenes, using images of the East.*

The collapse of Mongol power in the fourteenth century closed off the East to Europe once more. It was not until the sixteenth and seventeenth centuries, when European ships began to sail regularly to Southeast Asia and China, that more information on these lands became available. Some of the myths of the East were exposed as the fabrications they were, and scholars and academics became increasingly rigorous in the pursuit of factual accuracy in their studies of distant lands. But the more fanciful view of the Eastern lands remained popular. Travelers still told tall tales and the exquisite nature of the trade goods, such as Japanese lacquer, Chinese porcelain, and Indian fabrics, served to encourage ideas of strange lands — full of beauty, riches, and magic. They also helped to make the styles of the Orient extremely fashionable.

By the eighteenth century, the impact of Oriental goods and Western ideas of the East was being seen throughout Europe. Even landscape gardening was affected, resulting in a fashion propagated by the English known as *le jardin anglo-chinois.* Borrowing from Chinese gardens and paintings, a walk in *le jardin anglo-chinois* was designed to show a succession of views, as if a picture was slowly being unfurled. Trees, man-made lakes, and hills were carefully positioned to create different scenes for contemplation.

However, it was particularly in the visual arts and crafts that the new Eastern fashion was expressed, in a style known as "Chinoiserie." Chinoiserie was not an accurate representation of Chinese styles. The goods western craftsmen produced reflected an idealized image of the East and combined a multitude of different oriental styles with homegrown ones. Indian, Islamic, Chinese, and Japanese designs and motifs were happily adapted to western purposes, resulting in a style that was essentially European. Furniture, silver, ceramics, and textile designs were suffused with the spirit of chinoiserie.

The influence of the style can be detected in the work of artists such as Jean Watteau (1684–1721) and in some of the images of the Romantic movement in literature, such as the poems of Samuel Taylor Coleridge (1772–1824). Architecture, too, took on elements of these fanciful ideas. From the exotic *kiosques* of Louis XIV of France (1638–1715) and Frederick the Great of Prussia (1712–86) to the extraordinary Brighton Pavilion, built to please the whim of the Prince of Wales (later George VI, 1762–183), images of the Orient have produced buildings from the elegant to the bizarre.

▼ *Brighton Pavilion, England, designed by John Nash (1752–1835) for George, Prince of Wales at the end of the 18th century. It incorporates European ideas of Chinese, Indian, and Islamic architecture in a flamboyant mixture of styles.*

chapter seven

The Continuing Process

A New Impetus

▲ *"The Princess of the Country of Porcelain" (1864) by James Whistler. The influence of Japanese art is strong in this picture. Most importantly, the girl's stance echoes a print by Utamora, one of the greatest of the Japanese printmakers.*

▶ *Print by Japanese artist Katsushika Hokusai (1760–1849). It shows figures gazing at Mount Fuji in the distance. This element of perspective was a Western idea that was new to Japanese art. In turn, Hokusai's prints greatly influenced the works of the European Impressionists.*

It was the vast expansion of European trading links that led to the increasing impact of Eastern arts and crafts on Western styles. This expansion was given new impetus by the Industrial Revolution of the eighteenth and nineteenth centuries. The newly industrialized nations of Europe looked to Asia not only as a source of luxuries and raw materials, but, perhaps more importantly, as a lucrative market for selling their goods. The newly-formed United States now also joined the arena of international trade.

By the middle of the nineteenth century, the West's domination of world trade was no longer in question. Britain's defeat of China in the first Opium War (1839–42) had forced the reluctant Chinese to open more of their ports and cities to Western traders and, in 1853, the gunboats of the United States forced Japan to do the same. The old patterns of trade and cultural exchange embodied in the Silk and Spice Routes were completely submerged in the wholesale export of Western goods — and with them, Western culture.

Western ideas on economics, education, administration, and politics had a dramatic impact on the ancient cultures of Asia. Britain's control of India, which had begun as a result of trade, led to the imposition of its systems of administration and education. However, resistance to this process also produced an increased awareness of Indian nationality and culture. The new social and political movements that emerged in India were based on Western models, but also incorporated large elements of their own traditions.

In China, new Western ideas, combined with the pressure to compete commercially, undermined the ancient systems of administration and Empire. The ruling Qing Dynasty (1644–1912) resisted reform, leading to revolution in 1911. The Japanese, by contrast, once they had opened their doors fully to Western trade, embraced many elements of Western culture, too. Under the Meiji emperor (1867–1912), the old feudal system was abolished and administration was based around European models rather than the old Chinese ones that had been in operation since the seventh century A.D. Adopting Western technology and its capitalism, Japanese industry rapidly expanded and, by the end of the nineteenth century, its economy had long outstripped that of China.

In both East and West, these changes were reflected in art styles and images. Japanese artists were eager to learn about Western art and, at exhibitions held in Tokyo and Kyoto in the 1870s, any Western-style pieces exhibited sold quickly. In the West, Japanese art, such as the woodblock print, began to have a great effect. American artist James Whistler (1834–1903) borrowed ideas from the Japanese, and their use of light and color influenced the work of the European Impressionists. In architecture, too, the excesses of chinoiserie and other such styles were replaced by elements closer to the reality of Eastern style. The straight lines and uncluttered spaces of the interior designs and buildings of the Scottish architect Charles Rennie Mackintosh (1868–1928) echo the houses of Japan and Southeast Asia, revealing the wide assimilation of ideas that was taking place.

▼ *Façade of the Glasgow School of Art, designed 1907–9 by Charles Rennie Mackintosh. He was inspired partly by the architecture of Japan and Southeast Asia. The design contrasts spectacularly with the fanciful shapes of the Brighton Pavilion (see page 39).*

All Channels Open

▲ *"Fallingwater," a house designed by American architect Frank Lloyd Wright (1867–1959). He continued to develop ideas inspired by the architecture of Japan and Southeast Asia, closely relating buildings to their natural surroundings.*

The process of cultural exchange and assimilation by the peoples of the world continues to the present day. But the picture has become ever more complicated with the dramatic improvement in communications that has taken place. Airplanes, cars, telephones, televisions, and computers have made our world very different from that of a hundred years ago. Today, people have access to many different cultures through many different mediums and sometimes it is almost impossible to separate the various influences at work. Both East and West can share in the rich heritage and continuing innovations in their many different cultures.

Many Westerners live in open-plan apartments and work in open-plan offices, a concept that has developed partly from Eastern ideas of architecture and interior design. They may decorate these spaces with Turkish, Persian, Indian, and Chinese rugs or with ceramics by artists such as Bernard Leach and Lucie Rie, whose works have been inspired by the body shapes and colors of antique Chinese and Korean pottery. Eating out might be at a Thai, Chinese, or Japanese restaurant or. By buying a book or watching a television program, many learn how to cook these various cuisines for themselves. A trip to the ballet might involve watching work inspired by the Kabuki dances of Japan or *nritta* dances of India — or it could be to see one of the many Eastern dance companies on tour. Even the more modern trappings of a Westerner's life, such as the personal stereo or the computer, may well have been designed in Japan and manufactured in one of many Japanese-owned factories around the world.

On the other hand, Western influences in the East, particularly in Japan, are seen everywhere. Giant companies pay fortunes for European paintings, and many people wear Western clothes, jewelry, and hairstyles, and listen to Western music. Western dances and films are extremely popular, and Western literature, from the tragedies of Shakespeare to the comic strip, influence contemporary writers, playwrights, and film makers in Japan and other countries.

▲ Vase made by English potter Bernard Leach (1887–1979). Its design derives from older Eastern ceramics.

◄ There are many Eastern restaurants in the West today. Even more authentically, these people are eating in China.

▲ Scene from the film Ran by the Japanese film director Akira Kurosawa (1910–98). The film was inspired by King Lear, one of William Shakespeare's (1564–1616) tragedies.

The role of trade and commerce in this process is as important as ever. The global scale on which it is now practiced has been partly responsible for the development of an "international" sense of culture. It has also led to spectacular advances in industry and technology in many Asian countries, like Japan. Meanwhile, oil has given great wealth to many of the countries of the Middle East. Much of the world's wealth is still concentrated in Europe and the United States, but Asia is increasingly strong in finance as well.

Connecting
Past with Present

At the beginning of the twenty-first century, a nation's or people's culture is open to so many different influences that, in some cases, it seems a saturation point has been reached. Modern arts, crafts, and design have absorbed, adapted, and blended ideas from all over the world to the extent that it is perhaps difficult to speak of any "national" style. But many artists and craftsmen have consciously set out to maintain a sense of national or cultural identity in their work. They have been able to do this by looking to the traditions of the past for inspiration.

This process of linking past and present is not only apparent in the world of the creative arts. As ever, these are a reflection of influences at work in society as a whole. In a world of great change and uncertainty, people look to the past as a means of understanding the present and to give them a sense of continuity as well as identity. In Mongolia, which has emerged from the powerful influence of the former Soviet Union in the 1990s, people have turned again to Buddhism — while Genghis Khan, the builder of their massive empire in the thirteenth century, is widely celebrated. The national cultures of former old Soviet Central Asian states, such as Kazakhstan and Uzbekistan, have also emerged with renewed vigor — as well as old cultural and ethnic rivalries.

To understand the history of a single civilization or people, it is necessary to see the many different influences that have contributed to it. As the connections formed by the Silk and Spice Routes reveal, cultures and civilizations have not developed in isolation over the centuries, and it is partly because of this that there has been a renewed interest in the trade routes' history. Teams of scholars have traveled different sections of the Silk Route in China, central Asia, and Mongolia and along the Spice Routes from Italy to Japan. They have visited many historic sites and museums, working alongside academics from the local area. These expeditions have resulted in the setting up of international research programs, seminars, exhibitions, publications, and films. Projects like this not only to encourage a greater awareness of individual nations' pasts but also in the hope that, by revealing the heritage they share with others, it will be easier to maintain good international relations in the future.

◀ A camel caravan carrying tourists in the Gansu region of China. It was through this province of northwest China that the Silk Route passed. Today, tourists travel there to experience first-hand the path that was responsible for the development of such much of our common cultural heritage.

▲ A group of Mongol youths who have abandoned their horses, so much a part of their culture, for the attractions of a more modern form of transport — the motorbike.

A Silk and Spice Routes Time Chart

Date	Europe	Middle East & central Asia	China & the Far East
3000–0 B.C.	c. 3000 Minoan civilization, the earliest in Europe, develops in Crete. c. 1000–800 Greek speaking peoples move into Greece and begin to trade by sea throughout the Mediterranean. 753 Rome founded. c. 450 Athens emerges as the strongest city-state in Greece and the center of Greek cultural development. 336–323 Empire of Alexander the Great. Asian influences introduced into European culture. c. 250 Roman expansion begins. 146 Greece comes under Roman rule.	c. 3000 Egyptian hieroglyphics in use. c. 1500–600 Vedic Period in India, Hindu religion established. c. 500 Buddhism founded in China. 550–330 Achaemenid Empire of Persia. Zoroastrianism official state religion. Dynasty falls to Alexander, bringing Greek influences to Asia. 250–139 Graeco-Bactrian kingdom of Central Asia. 247–170 Parthians establish their Persian Empire. 200s Buddhism begins to spread north. Gandhara art style emerges.	c. 3000 Silk first produced in China. c. 2205–1766 Xia Dynasty in China. First use of written symbols. c. 1766–1027 Shang dynasty in China. 1027–221 Zhou dynasty in China. 221–206 Qin dynasty unites whole of China for first time. 202 Han dynasty founded. Further develops a sophisticated civil service to administer its vast empire. c. 100 Han empire expands in Tarim region of central Asia. Enables Silk Route to operate right across Asia, connecting China with the West.
A.D. 1–500	A.D. 117 Roman Empire at its largest; a major market for Eastern goods. 310–337 Reign of Emperor Constantine. Christianity adopted as official Roman religion. Constantinople replaces Rome as capital. 395 Roman Empire splits into two. 476 Western Roman Empire collapses. 486 Frankish kingdom, with lands in Germany and France, formed.	C. A.D. 29 Death of Jesus Christ. Spread of Christianity begins. c. 70–224 Kushan Empire of Central Asia. Sogidans trading on Silk Route. 224 Sasanians seize power from Parthians. Their empire a strong cultural influence along trade routes. c. 276 Death of Mani in Persia. Manichaeism spreads through Asia and Europe. Dies out by 14th century.	A.D. 100 First Buddhist conversions in China. 220 Hans Dynasty collapses. China fragments into three. 316–598 Rival dynasties in north and south China. 300s Secret of sericulture begins to spread west along the Silk Route. c. 400 Chinese script introduced into Japan.
501–1000	610 Roman Empire now focused around eastern Mediterranean; known as Byzantine Empire. 711 Arabs conquer Spain. 793–94 Vikings begin to raid northern Europe. 800 Charlemagne crowned Emperor of a new Frankish Western (later Holy Roman) Empire. 800s Venice formed as a city-state.	500s Turks establish empire across northern Asia, taking in Sogdian territories. Sogdians still trade. 622 The religion of Islam founded. 632 Death of Muhammad. Muslim Arab expansion begins. 651 Sasanian Persia falls to the Arabs. Islamic culture developing with Sasanian and Byzantine influences. mid-900s Muslim Empire fragments	552 Buddhism introduced into Japan. 589 Sui dynasty reunites China. 618–907 Tang dynasty rules in China. For first two centuries, Buddhism flourishes and China very open to foreign cultural influences. 794–1185 Heian Period in Japan. 800s First porcelain made in China. 907–76 China divided by civil wars. 976 Sung dynasty reunites China.
1001–1400	1001 Start of Medieval Period. 1096–1291 European Christians undertake crusades to regain the Holy Land from its Muslim rulers. 1100s Silk production and weaving established in Italy. 1236 Mongols invade Russia. 1271 Marco Polo sets out for the East.	1260–1368 Mongols control Central and much of western Asia. Silk Route trade prospers under Pax Mongolica. 1281–1326 Reign of Osman I, founder of Turkish Ottoman Empire. 1325–48 Ibn Battuta travels throughout Asia.	1126 China divided into two. 1196 Ghengis Khan unites Mongols. Expansion of Mongol Empire begins. 1227 Death of Ghengis Kahn. 1264 Kublai Khan founds Mongol Yuan dynasty in China. 1368 Yuan dynasty overthrown and replaced by Chinese Ming dynasty.
1401–1750	c. 1401 Renaissance period begins. 1453 Constantine falls to Ottoman Turks. Byzantine Empire ends. 1488 Bartolomeu Dias sails round the southern tip of Africa. 1492 All Muslim power in Spain ends. 1492 Columbus reaches America. 1497–99 Vasco de Gama sails from Portugal via Africa to India. c. 1600 Dutch and English begin to trade directly with India and beyond. c. 1750 The start of the European Industrial Revolution.	1405 Death of Tamerlane marks final collapse of Mongol power. Silk Route no longer operates internationally. 1500s Gradual decline of trade routes linking the Indian Ocean with the Mediterranean. 1510 Portuguese capture Goa on west coast of India. 1526–1857 Muslim Mughal dynasty of India. Encourages European trade. 1566 Ottoman Empire at its largest. 1594 English first trade with India, the start of their influence there.	1405–33 Chinese explore the Spice Routes as far as Africa. c. 1450 Chinese adopt an isolationist foreign policy. Discourages trade. 1511 Portuguese take the Spice Route port of Malaka. 1570–1637 Nagasaki, Japan, open to foreign traders. After this brief period Japan closed to foreigners until 1853. 1596 Dutch arrive in East Indies 1644–1912 Qing (Manchu) dynasty rules China. Limited foreign trade until forced to open ports in 1842.

Glossary

Axum Ancient African kingdom that flourished in the first to sixth centuries CE and covered a large part of modern Ethiopia as well as the Sudan.

Bactria Former name for a region of central Asia centered around the city of Bactria (Balk) in modern Afghanistan. It was ruled for a while by a Greek dynasty established by the conquests of Alexander the Great in the fourth century B.C.

Boccaccio, Giovanni Italian poet (1313-75), born in Florence, mainly known for his collection of tales called the *Decameron*.

Buddhism A religious path taught in India by Siddhartha Gautama (c.560-483 B.C.), known as the Buddha. It declares that by understanding the origins of all human suffering, people can reach perfect enlightenment or *nirvana*.

caravanserai A large inn enclosing a courtyard providing shelter and accommodation for caravans or travelers and their camels or other pack animals.

Caxton, William The first English printer (c.1422-91). Born in Kent, he learned the art of printing in Cologne and then set up a press in Belgium where he produced the first book printed in English. He returned to England in 1476 and established himself in London.

Christianity The religion founded in Palestine by the followers of Jesus of Nazareth (c. 5 B.C.-A.D.29), later known as Jesus Christ. His teachings spread rapidly throughout the Roman Empire until Christianity became the official state religion towards the end of the fourth century A.D.

Hinduism The religion established in India during the Verdic Period (c. 1500-600 B.C.). It is characterized by the worship of many gods, including Brahma as the supreme being, and the belief in reincarnation.

Ibn Battuta Arab traveller (1304-68) born in Tangiers, Morocco. In 1325 he left on an incredible 74,818 mile journey via Mecca to Egypt, then on to East Africa, India, and China. He returned home briefly only to depart for Spain and to cross the Sahara. His travels took 30 years to complete.

Impressionism A movement in painting that began in France in the 1860s and dominated European and North American painting in the late 19th century. The Impressionists wanted to paint straight from nature and capture the changing effects of light. Famous artists in the movement include Monet, Renoir, Sisley, Cezanne, Manet, and Degas.

incense Once very rare and costly, it is made from various sweet-smelling substances, usually the sap from certain plants and trees. Myrrh and frankincense are the most famous. Crystals of the dried sap are sprinkled on to hot coals and they produce a perfumed smoke. Spices and fragrant woods are also sometimes burned as incense.

Islam This means literally "surrender" (to God). Islam is a religion founded by Muhammad (c. A.D.570-632) whose followers became known as Muslims. The *Qur'an* (Koran) is Islam's sacred scripture which teaches that there is only one God and that Muhammad is His prophet.

Kushan A people of Central Asia who ruled over most of northern India and Afghanistan during the first three centuries A.D. They played an active part in the Silk Route trade. They were also instrumental in spreading Buddhism into central Asia.

Manichaeism The religion founded in A.D. 241 in Persia by the prophet Mani (c. 216-276). It spread throughout Europe and Asia until about the 10th Century, despite persecution. It held that the material world is evil and is an invasion of the spiritual world of light by the powers of darkness.

Marco Polo A Venetian merchant (1254-1324), famous for his account of his travels in Asia. After traveling overland to China (1271-75) with his father and uncle, he spent 17 years serving the Mongol emperor of China, Kublai Kahn, before returning to Venice by sea (1292-5).

Maurya dynasty Indian royal dynasty (c. 321-185 B.C.). Under the Mauryan emperor Asoka, most of India was united for the first time, but his empire broke up following his death in 232.

monsoon This is the seasonal wind of southern Asia that blows from the southwest during the summer months bringing heavy rains, and blows from the northeast during the winter.

motif A central image or figure used in art or design.

Mughals An Indian dynasty of emperors (1526-1857) founded by Babur. They were Muslim descendants of Tamerlane and ruled until the last emperor was finally dethroned and exiled by the British in 1857.

Muslims See *Islam*.

Parthians A people from the area southeast of the Caspian Sea in Asia. They controlled a great empire in western Asia from the second century B.C. Weakened by internal feuds and attacks from Roman armies, the Parthian Empire fell to the Sasanians in A.D. 224.

Persia The name given to Iran until 1935.

porcelain A very fine ceramic or pottery ware. It is sometimes known as china, as it was the Chinese who developed the technique of making porcelain some time before A.D. 900.

Sasanians The ruling people of Iran from A.D. 224, after their defeat of the Parthians. Over the next 400 years, the Sasanians controlled Persia (Iran) and other areas of western Asia, until they in turn fell before Arab armies in A.D. 642.

silk The very fine fiber produced by the silkmoth caterpillar when it makes its cocoon. Silken twine is made from the fibers and this can be woven to make fabrics. The craft of producing silk and its cloth is known as sericulture.

Scythians A nomadic people who occupied a region to the north of the Black Sea around the eighth and fourth centuries B.C. They are famous for their ornaments of gold and electrum (a natural alloy of gold and silver) with animal decoration.

Sogdians A people who occupied the region of Central Asia around the modern city of Samarkand. Because of their strategic position on the main East-West trade routes, they formed an important link in the chain of cultural exchange. Sogdiana remained a prosperous center until the Mongol invasions.

Tamerlane Turkish ruler, also known as Timur the Lame (1336-1405), who claimed descent from the Mongols and built an empire centered around his capital of Samarkand. This took in territories from Persia, Azerbaijan, Armenia, and Georgia. This empire crumbled on his death, but his heirs went on to found the Mughal Empire in India.

Turks Natives of Turkey, but the name is also applied to Turkic-speaking people as a whole. The Turks originated in Central Asia but pushed westward into Byzantine territories during the 15th century. They established their own empire, known as the Ottoman Empire (after the ruling Ottoman Dynasty) throughout the Middle East and Balkan region of Europe.

Zoroastrianism Religion named after the prophet Zoroaster who lived in Persia during the seventh Century B.C., and still practiced by the Parsis in India. Worship is made at altars where a sacred fire burns. The religion is based on the concept of a constant struggle between good and evil.

Index

Acknowledgements

Ancient Art and Architecture Collection 16 top, 17, 34 left, 35 right; Architectural Association 41 © Valerie Bennett; Bibliotéque Nationale 8, 10 center top, 35 left, 37 center; Bridgeman Art Library 15 right and 37 top (British Library), 23 top (Hanley Museum & Art Gallery, Staffordshire). 38 top (Victoria & Albert Museum, London); British Museum 6 top, 11 bottom, 12 bottom, 18, 22 left; Commercial Press (Hong Kong) Ltd from the publication "Chinese Textile Design" 24 top; © Comstock Inc/Anthony Howarth cover; Crafts Council 43 top; E.T. Archive 13 top (Victoria & Albert Museum, London), 27 bottom (Hermitage, St Petersburg), 33 top (British Library); Freer Gallery of Art, Smithsonian Institution, Washington 46.12 (fol.5): 15 right, D.C. 03.91: 40 top; The Ronald Grant Archive 43 center right © Nippon Herald Films Inc; Sonia Halliday Photographs 26 center; Robert Harding 9 top, 13 bottom, 20 bottom left, 25 center, 26 top, 28 bottom, 30/31, 39, 42, 43 center left, 44/45; Roland & Sabrina Michaud from The John Hillelson Agency 14 top; Hutchison Library right 34 © John Hatt; Metropolitan Museum of Art, Purchase, Rogers Fund and The Kevorkian Foundations Gift, 1955. (55.121.10.23): 21, Bequest of Mary Stillman Harkness, 1950: 30 bottom left; Toby Molenaar 10 bottom, 20 top; Musée des Arts Décoratifs, Paris, L.Sully-Jaulmes page 25 top; Museum Yamoto Benkakan, Nara, Japan 32 right; Natural History Museum, London 7 top; NY Carlsberg Glyptotek, Copenhagen 14 bottom, 27 top; Österreichisches Nationalbibliotek, Vienna 28 top; Rijksmuseum voor Volkakunde, Leiden 40 bottom; RMN 19 top and 22 right (Musée Guimet), 24 center (Musée Cluny); Royal Ontario Museum 29 top; Scala 20 bottom right; Seattle Art Museum, Eugene Fuller Memorial Collection, 37.17 10 topleft; Staatliche Museen zu Berlin - Preßischer Kulturbesitz Museum für Indische Kunst 32 left; State Hermitage Museum, St Petersburg, Russia 11 top; Topkapi Palace Museum 23 bottom; UNESCO/Silk Roads Photograph donated by the photographer to the "Integral Study of the Silk Roads: Roads of Dialogue" 7 bottom, 31 bottom right and 45 inset (Toby Molenaar), 10/11, 16 bottom (Anne Garde), 26 bottom (Earl Kowall); Werner Forman Archive 6 bottom, 9 bottom (National Palace Museum, Taipi), 12 top, 19 bottom, 33 bottom (Earl Morse Coll., Metropolitan Museum of Art, New York)